We should all be wealthy: The ultimate guide for overcoming a full house wife mindset.

Table of Content

Chapter 1

INTRODUCTION

Why You Should Be Rich (3 Big Reasons you should be rich)

Many individuals have difficulty with money. And if you have a deeply entrenched conviction that money is "evil" then I promise it's the ONE thing standing in your way of having more of it, no matter what you do in your career.
So, what's your relationship with money?

Here I am going to list 3 precise reasons you should be wealthy – and explain how if you're not affluent, you're selling yourself short.
But first, I want to emphasize how arbitrary the notion of money is.
It's merely a tool that somewhere down the line our ancestors chose to employ to trade value.

If you think about it, back in the day, instead of using real money, people swapped commodities that had value to them - cattle, food, or anything they had that another person desired or needed. But today, it's all about paper money.

The underlying reality of all this is the fact that many of us have a hangup when it comes to money since we've been conditioned — whether it's through our parents, schools, churches, or society in general – to believe that being rich is bad.

For instance, in many movies, the affluent person is typically a villain. And Robin Hood, who takes from the affluent and gives to the needy, is presented as a heroic guy.

That's such a fallacy. It's backward, since having money is vital when it comes to your quality of life. If you want a great home, if you want to have more options, it's vital to have money. Every successful entrepreneur knows (and believes) this.

No one gains from you being impoverished.

And no amount of depriving yourself of money would ever lead others to a better degree of prosperity themselves.

The finest thing you can do for your own life and others around you is to be plentiful — in all parts of your life.

3 Reasons You Deserve to Be Rich

I want to offer you a small perspective change here.

You were not placed in this world to be impoverished. Being impoverished doesn't benefit anyone, and that's the first thing I want you to realize.

Being impoverished is not noble. It's selling yourself — and everyone around you – short. Let me show you why...

1. You Can Help More People

The more money you generate, the more profit you have in your firm, and that extra profit mean you can offer more to the world.

Now think of any philanthropists, they all operate a profitable company that's why they can touch life's
It seems easy, the more money you have the more you can touch people around the globe.
Now, think about the individuals you wish to serve. You can't assist them if you don't have any money, right? If you want to produce a change in the world, it needs money.
Which indicates that you need to be a little bit wealthy. Being poor and being broke does not assist anyone, particularly yourself.

2. It Comes as a result of Your Personal Growth
This is a multi-pronged reason you should be affluent. I frequently encourage individuals that they should try to become a multi-millionaire ... but it's not always because of the money.
It's because of who you become in the process.

This personal growth happens in a multitude of ways, and I'm going to detail three of them.
There are very evident contrasts between someone who is making millions of dollars vs someone who flips hamburgers at McDonald's. Now, I'm not claiming one is better than the

other, not at all. But there is a distinction in terms of personal progress.

First, you learn to offer value.

The reason the worker flipping hamburgers at McDonald's is getting a minimum wage is that pretty much anyone can perform that job. Maybe in the not-so-distant future, a robot will probably do it.

But the reason top-level entrepreneurs, CEOs, thinkers, and artists make so much money is that relatively few people can accomplish what they do. They add a particular value to the market, and that's why they are paid big wages.

And the reason they can contribute that value is that they went through a path of development, growth, and learning that allowed them to gain the talents and assets that make them incredibly valuable to society.
If you want to generate more money, give something that is valued. And be so excellent that few people can even compete with you.

Meanwhile, the individual flipping burgers — whether they're 15 or 30, or 50 years old – hasn't gone through the same evolutionary route to give greater value to the workplace.
I can't bear it when people whine about the fact that they're not generating enough money.

Here's the reality check:

If you were to ask me for a raise, I'd answer by asking you why. If you desire the increase, you should be prepared to present some concrete instances of how you are delivering value.

There are two lessons there: one, you have to ask for an increase and second, you have to establish your value.

If you want more money, become more useful to the people you serve, whether that's your client base or a firm that you're working with.
Until you become more valued, you won't earn more money.
Can you see how you become a more valued person in the process of obtaining more money?

Money is not the end-all, but in terms of contributing more value and riches to the world, you first have to become a creator – since all money follows value. Value is just creation –something you thought of and made, whether it's a book, product, or idea.
Second, you become a conqueror, not a victim.
Victims cry that the world is against them.
Creators, on the other hand, take responsibility for their lives. They're conquerors. They say: "Things may not be the way I want them to be, but I am going to be accountable for changing them to how I want them."

That is how you generate value in this world. It's not through having a "poor me" mindset.
Third, you learn to handle your money carefully.
There's a spiritual saying that you should be able to handle the tiny things before you can acquire the great things.

For instance, if you want three scoops of ice cream on your cone, you should make sure that you can manage one without it slipping off first.

The same principle can be applied to practically everything in life - including money. Manage the tiny before you acquire the huge. If you handle the modest amounts, that'll make it simpler to amass the bigger ones.

It's who you become in a way to becoming affluent that's the most important thing.
It's not about winning the lotto. You've undoubtedly heard that most lottery winners lose all their money shortly after they win their jackpots, right?

That's because one day they wake up as their daily selves, with all of their normal thoughts, behaviors, and beliefs.
And then they wake up the following day, and they've won $40 million ... yet they are still the same person with the same ideas, behaviors, and beliefs. They haven't had a chance to develop and they haven't gone through the trip that is necessary to help them hang on to that money.

They're probably going out and purchasing pricey stuff that is nothing but toys and has no worth.

That's why I've always claimed that I don't want to win the lotto since it ruins the voyage. The journey is what counts, not the outcome.

Go through the road of becoming a multi-millionaire. You will be far better off when you reflect on your life than someone who merely stumbles into money. I guarantee it.

3. You Can Live a Better Life

The third reason why you should be affluent is that you may enhance your quality of life.

If you have kids, they have access to better schools and better meals. You're able to live where you want to reside and have a nicer home. And you may enjoy tiny pleasures, like traveling first-class instead of coach.

Never feel terrible about these "better" things. Never allow other people to make you feel guilty about having the goods and living the life you want to live.

You are intended to have it all. You may appreciate the nicer things in life - there's nothing wrong with that.
The reality is when individuals attempt to make you feel guilty what they're truly saying is that they don't believe they deserve those things. Don't allow their bullshit to get into your brain.

Now, I live in the home of my dreams. I have my dream automobile. And I have my children — and I adore all I have.
I'm well conscious of the fact that my home and my vehicle are mere "things," but when it comes to material stuff, they are pretty much the only two things that I care about.

For me, what's most important are the connections I have and the value that I give out into this world, and I never get them confused.

Don't assume that if you have the money, you should feel awful about purchasing items you genuinely desire. You can have your toys - by all means, you're here in this world to enjoy it. But at the same time recognize that they are not going to make you happy.

It's the other way around: You have to be happy first before that thing enters into your life. Concentrate on what counts in your life, which again is not the surface rubbish.

Overcome Your Limiting Thoughts

Those are the three reasons why I believe you should be wealthy.

If you have a problem with money, it's a personal journey that you have to work on. Do everything you can to increase your self-worth, coupled with your affiliation and relationship with money.

All of that is more extensive than what I can address in this essay, but focusing on self-development, such as attending a Tony Robbins "Unleash the Power Within" event, or similar programs may go a long way toward overcoming your limiting beliefs.

Then, you'll be ready to elevate yourself to a more powerful position, which may make a significant impact.

Chapter 2

EXCUSES TO LET GO OF

- That you are not a goal oriented person
- That you don't have time(instead manage the time you have)
- That you are not enough to succeed
- Afraid of failure and think you have try so many things

1: Believing that you are not goal oriented.

When it comes to reaching objectives, most individuals lack one key character to achieve their goals, which is that they are not goal focused enough. They establish and write down their objectives once, and then they allow everything to happen by chance. They do not examine their objectives, they do not plan, and they do not measure their progress.

As a consequence, people lose sight of their objectives, which ultimately leads them to lose the interest they have in their ambitions. And towards the end, they quit and give up on their ambitions.
If this is occurring to you right now, you need to do something about it. You need to learn to be more goal focused in life.

Highly successful individuals like Elon Musk, Steve Jobs, Bill Gates, Mark Cuban, etc, are utterly goal-focused. They can't stop thinking about the things that they want to attain, they have their objectives in their thoughts all the time, and they continually work ceaselessly toward what they desire. And this is why they can generate exceptional success in life.

How to Become More Goal Oriented in Your Life.

1. Plan Your Day

The first thing you need to do to become more goal-oriented is to arrange your day. Without preparation, there is no way you can ensure that you are going to make progress on your objectives.

We all are busy and distractions are around. Hence, without preparation for our day, we would be lost in our day-to-day operations and wonder where the time goes.

While it is true that your day may not turn out precisely as you had planned, having a plan is still far better than having no plan at all. When you have a plan, you understand what you need to get done. In other words, you are proactive.

On the other side, when you have no strategy, you will become reactive because you will respond to whatever things that thrown at you. For instance, if you have no clue what to do during the weekend, and when your friends invite you for a drink, there is a great possibility that you would agree because you believe that you are free and have nothing to do anyway.

However, if you already have a strategy, things will be drastically different. This is why planning is crucial. Thus, write down what you need to get done for the day each morning before you start your day.

2. Schedule Your Actions

The second thing you can do to become more goal-oriented is to plan your activities. Studies have shown that when we schedule the task, we considerably boost the possibility that it will happen.

Scheduling is like scheduling an appointment with oneself. For example, if you want to go to the gym and exercise for an hour, simply arrange it as a timetable and tell yourself, “I’m going to the gym at 7 AM this Sunday and I will work out from 7:30 AM to 9 AM, for one and a half hour.”

When you arrange your assignment in this manner, you are making your task to become extremely precise, which boosts the clarity of how your mind can perform the activity.

Therefore, you may arrange most of the work and activities that you are going to undertake to make progress toward your objectives.

You may always start with your calendar and also your to-do list. Schedule your to-do list items so that you will know precisely when and where to carry out the activity. Furthermore, you can also utilize a calendar and put down ad-hoc activities that you wish to act on.

If you're enjoying this post, be sure to check out our collection of words of wisdom to bring out the best in you.

3. Review Your Progress
One of the primary reasons individuals are not goal-oriented and they fail to attain their objectives is because they did not assess their progress.

A lot of individuals felt that goal setting is a one-time procedure wherein they simply need to jot down their objectives once, and then the results would come to them naturally, this is untrue.

Goal setting is a continual process where you need to regularly analyze your progress and actively monitor your outcomes.

Whatever is out of your sight will be out of your thoughts. Thus, you must regularly examine your objectives to remind yourself of what you want to accomplish and what you need to do to get there.

Let's Get Real About Achieving Goals And Making In Happen

Another major reason you want to routinely examine your objectives is that you want to train your goals in your subconscious mind. Most individuals fail to create the outcomes they desire because they did not evaluate their objectives, which makes them forget about their aims, and then they lose their love for the goals, which finally, makes them give up.

So do not allow this to happen to you. Make it a habit to evaluate your objectives every day.

4. Follow the 90/90/1 Rule

This powerful guideline is offered by the acclaimed and best-selling author, Robin Sharma. He added that if you want to be goal-oriented and achieve success in life, simply commit to the 90/90/1 Rule.

This guideline indicates that for the following 90 days, spend 90 minutes each day performing 1 activity that advances you toward your objectives.

If your objective is to develop a successful blog, find out what is the one thing you can do to advance and attain your goal. And most likely, that one thing for bloggers will be posting great material. Thus, commit to the 90/90/1 Rule by creating great content for 90 minutes each day for the following 90 days.

You may apply this guideline to every other aspect of your life. If you want to lose weight, figure out the one thing that you can do to drop the weight, and then commit to performing the task for 90 minutes a day for the next 90 days. Just follow the 90/90/1 Rule like what Robin Sharma stated.

5. Network and Mix with the Right People
Jim Rohn was accurate when he observed, "You are the average of the five individuals you spend the most time with." If you want to be goal

focused, simply mix and network with others who are likewise goals minded.
Goal-oriented folks will speak a lot about their goals, their aspirations, and how are they going to get there. They are enthusiastic to discuss their aims and aspirations, and they are ready to share their opinions with you.

When you talk to other people, the topic of conversation is important because it will influence your thinking. Unsuccessful individuals typically speak about other people, they blame others, and they often make reasons for why accomplishing things are difficult.

The first step you need to do is to quit or drastically minimize your time spent with negative individuals. And the second stage is to network and mingle with other goal-driven individuals.

6. Write It Down

This is the most frequent error that most people never do. They underestimated the significance of putting down their ambitions.

When you set down your objectives into papers, it simply demonstrates that you are dedicated enough and are serious about accomplishing them. This is why you bother writing them down. People who are not serious and are not devoted to their objectives will never bother to write them down in the first place.

This is a significant contrast between someone who is dedicated and someone who is not. Plus, when you write down your objectives, you are reminding your subconscious mind that these are essential concepts that you love to reach.

And guess what, your subconscious mind will then goes to work 24/7 to come up with ideas and give you the initiative to work on the objectives.

What you need to do is easy, simply jot down your objectives each day. And make it your habit to do so. Remember, you want to implant the concept of attaining your objectives in your subconscious.

7. Be 100 percent Committed

Finally, if you want to be more goal-oriented, you must treat your objectives with 100 percent devotion. This is where a lot of individuals fail, particularly when the situation gets harsh, they opt to quit their ambitions.

For instance, if you want to train at the gym each morning, choose to be 100 percent devoted and follow your plan. Regardless matter whether it rains or not. Many individuals opt to cease taking action when they meet a hurdle such as rain. They opt to stay to sleep in their nice and warm bed rather than get up and act on their aspirations.

Goal-oriented individuals are persons who are devoted to reaching their objectives. They are prepared to do whatever it takes to get there. Are you?

When it comes to reaching objectives, most individuals lack one key character to achieve their goals, which is that they are not goal focused enough. They establish and write down their objectives once, and then they allow everything to happen by chance. They do not examine their objectives, they do not plan, and they do not measure their progress.

As a consequence, people lose sight of their objectives, which ultimately leads them to lose the interest they have in their ambitions. And towards the end, they quit and give up on their ambitions.
If this is occurring to you right now, you need to do something about it. You need to learn to be more goal focused in life.

Highly successful individuals like Elon Musk, Steve Jobs, Bill Gates, Mark Cuban, etc, are utterly goal-focused. They can't stop thinking about the things that they want to attain, they have their objectives in their thoughts all the time, and they continually work ceaselessly toward what they desire. And this is why they can generate exceptional success in life.

How to Become More Goal Oriented in Your Life.

1. Plan Your Day

The first thing you need to do to become more goal-oriented is to arrange your day. Without preparation, there is no way you can ensure that you are going to make progress on your objectives.

We all are busy and distractions are around. Hence, without preparation for our day, we would be lost in our day-to-day operations and wonder where the time goes.

While it is true that your day may not turn out precisely as you had planned, having a plan is still far better than having no plan at all. When you have a plan, you understand what you need to get done. In other words, you are proactive.

On the other side, when you have no strategy, you will become reactive because you will respond to whatever things that thrown at you. For instance, if you have no clue what to do during the weekend, and when your friends invite you for a drink, there is a great possibility that you would agree because you believe that you are free and have nothing to do anyway. However, if you already have a strategy, things will be drastically different. This is why planning is crucial. Thus, write down what you need to get done for the day each morning before you start your day.

2. Schedule Your Actions

The second thing you can do to become more goal-oriented is to plan your activities. Studies have shown that when we schedule the task, we considerably boost the possibility that it will happen.

Scheduling is like scheduling an appointment with oneself. For example, if you want to go to the gym and exercise for an hour, simply arrange it as a timetable and tell yourself, “I’m going to the gym at 7 AM this Sunday and I will work out from 7:30 AM to 9 AM, for one and a half hour.”

When you arrange your assignment in this manner, you are making your task to become extremely precise, which boosts the clarity of how your mind can perform the activity.

Therefore, you may arrange most of the work and activities that you are going to undertake to make progress toward your objectives.

You may always start with your calendar and also your to-do list. Schedule your to-do list items so that you will know precisely when and where to carry out the activity. Furthermore, you can also utilize a calendar and put down ad-hoc activities that you wish to act on.

If you're enjoying this post, be sure to check out our collection of words of wisdom to bring out the best in you.

3. Review Your Progress
One of the primary reasons individuals are not goal-oriented and they fail to attain their objectives is because they did not assess their progress.

A lot of individuals felt that goal setting is a one-time procedure wherein they simply need to jot down their objectives once, and then the results would come to them naturally, this is untrue.

Goal setting is a continual process where you need to regularly analyze your progress and actively monitor your outcomes.
Whatever is out of your sight will be out of your thoughts. Thus, you must regularly examine your objectives to remind yourself of what you want to accomplish and what you need to do to get there.

Let's Get Real About Achieving Goals And Making In Happen
Another major reason you want to routinely examine your objectives is that you want to train your goals in your subconscious mind. Most individuals fail to create the outcomes they desire because they did not evaluate their objectives, which makes them forget about their

aims, and then they lose their love for the goals, which finally, makes them give up.
So do not allow this to happen to you. Make it a habit to evaluate your objectives every day.

4. Follow the 90/90/1 Rule
This powerful guideline is offered by the acclaimed and best-selling author, Robin Sharma. He added that if you want to be goal-oriented and achieve success in life, simply commit to the 90/90/1 Rule.

This guideline indicates that for the following 90 days, spend 90 minutes each day performing 1 activity that advances you toward your objectives.
If your objective is to develop a successful blog, find out what is the one thing you can do to advance and attain your goal. And most likely, that one thing for bloggers will be posting great material. Thus, commit to the 90/90/1 Rule by creating great content for 90 minutes each day for the following 90 days.

You may apply this guideline to every other aspect of your life. If you want to lose weight, figure out the one thing that you can do to drop the weight, and then commit to performing the task for 90 minutes a day for the next 90 days.

Just follow the 90/90/1 Rule like what Robin Sharma stated.

5. Network and Mix with the Right People
Jim Rohn was accurate when he observed, "You are the average of the five individuals you spend the most time with." If you want to be goal focused, simply mix and network with others who are likewise goals minded.

Goal-oriented folks will speak a lot about their goals, their aspirations, and how are they going to get there. They are enthusiastic to discuss their aims and aspirations, and they are ready to share their opinions with you.

When you speak to other people, the subject of discussion is vital since it will affect your thoughts. Unsuccessful individuals typically speak about other people, they blame others, and they often make reasons for why accomplishing things are difficult.

The first step you need to do is to quit or drastically minimize your time spent with negative individuals. And the second stage is to network and mingle with other goal-driven individuals.

6. Write It Down

This is the most frequent error that most people never do. They underestimated the significance of putting down their ambitions.

When you set down your objectives into papers, it simply demonstrates that you are dedicated enough and are serious about accomplishing them. This is why you bother writing them down. People who are not serious and are not devoted to their objectives will never bother to write them down in the first place.

This is a significant contrast between someone who is dedicated and someone who is not. Plus, when you write down your objectives, you are reminding your subconscious mind that these are essential concepts that you love to reach.

And guess what, your subconscious mind will then goes to work 24/7 to come up with ideas and give you the initiative to work on the objectives.

What you need to do is easy, simply jot down your objectives each day. And make it your habit to do so. Remember, you want to implant the concept of attaining your objectives in your subconscious.

7. Be 100 percent Committed

Finally, if you want to be more goal-oriented, you must treat your objectives with 100 percent devotion. This is where a lot of individuals fail, particularly when the situation gets harsh, they opt to quit their ambitions.

For instance, if you want to train at the gym each morning, choose to be 100 percent devoted and follow your plan. Regardless matter whether it rains or not. Many individuals opt to cease taking action when they meet a hurdle such as rain. They opt to stay to sleep in their nice and warm bed rather than get up and act on their aspirations.

Goal-oriented individuals are persons who are devoted to reaching their objectives. They are prepared to do whatever it takes to get there. Are you?

2: Believing that you don't have time (Instead manage your time)

As women and parents, we naturally have a strong work ethic and the capacity to keep a hectic schedule. But the expanding group of female entrepreneurs is seeking to take things to the next level. Which may make anybody feel stressed. Feeling like nothing is ever truly done.

Working 24/7/365 isn't an indication of great time management. In reality, it's an indication of a lack of time management. You need time for resting, relaxing, family time, and socializing.

Thus, time management isn't about quantity. You can't evaluate success by the number of hours you worked. Instead, you need to start evaluating how productive and influential those hours were.

If you're ready to start working smarter, try implementing these seven techniques into your routine.

1 – Have a Plan A and a Plan B (and even a Plan C) (and even a Plan C)
Bullet journal calendar layout
Bullet journaling is a terrific method to become organized!
There is no such thing as a typical week. But it doesn't mean you shouldn't have a strategy.

Creating Plan A covers what you anticipate doing during the week.

Develop a list of priorities, schedule appointments, and keep note of occurrences on your calendar.
Plan everything. This lets you determine how to assign your time to each priority, appointment, and event. Don't devote more time to a job than you believe it requires — work fills the available space.
But, things don't always go as planned. So it helps to have a mental Plan B to give oneself license to pivot without feeling bad about the regular disruptions of life. To construct a Plan B, remember:

You don't need to write anything down since you may not need it, therefore you don't want to waste all your time generating numerous lists. Just go through your triage list - What has to be done if your time for work is severely cut down? If something unexpected happens, Plan B lets you alter your priority list to remain on target.
And, if anything huge comes up, take Plan C up from the back of your mind where you store your disaster preparedness list.

It may seem like a lot to write down or contemplate. But these lists keep you focused and calm even when the week looks to be going south.

2. Work in a block instead than multitasking.

Time management theory is used to teach the advantages of multitasking. But, what happens when you multitask is you typically spend a lot of time doing very little (and not so effectively) (and not so well).

You are spreading your focus and skills among two or more projects. And that's a formula for blunders. In the end, you may have to spend more time repairing such problems.

Instead, employ the Pomodoro Technique, often known as time blocking. Here's how it works:

Choose the first item on your priority list. Then, set the clock for 25 minutes and work within that time restriction to get it done. That means

no checking email, answering the phone, or stealing a peek at social media.
When the timer goes off, quit that task, and take a little rest.
Either set the timer again to continue that job or proceed to the next item on your list.
That laser concentration helps you to tick tasks off quicker and with greater vigor.

3 – Require Work-Life Balance
Family calendar organizer

A common school of thinking puts work first and expects everything else will fall into place around employment. But it's time to stop thinking that the personal portions of our life are diversions.

Instead, put the person first. Planning work around family, friends, and "me" time.

And, if anything huge comes up, take Plan C up from the back of your mind where you store your disaster preparedness list.

It may seem like a lot to write down or contemplate. But these lists keep you focused and calm even when the week looks to be going south.

4 – Get an App For That (and Everything Else) (and Everything Else)
Hurdlr software to help manage business costs
Hurdlr is a great tool for effortlessly monitoring business and side hustle revenue, expenditures, and tax deductions!

Replace multitasking with automation. Thanks to applications, you eliminate additional time-consuming, hard job duties off your plate. Not sure what to automate?

Start with monthly bills and recurrent spending and invoices. Hurdlr can arrange your company costs and taxes to save you time and money.
Use a calendar tool that also automates appointments, meetings, and events. Meetingbird allows you to bypass the back and forth when attempting to plan a meeting by enabling several participants to put in available

times and automatically arranging at a time that works for everyone.
Use Asana to keep track of all your tasks and operate more effectively with workers or contractors.
Add linked gadgets that aid with supplies, shopping orders, and other boring duties.
5 – Give Yourself a Break
Cozy slippers of someone napping - Entrepreneurs must take breaks.

Some entrepreneurs proclaim that they took their "lunch" at their work to get more done. That's not impressive.
No one should look down on you for walking away from work. Everyone's brain and body need a getaway. That's why breaks were developed, among other reasons.

Use the time for stretching or a brisk stroll. This activity boosts blood flow to the brain so you think better. It's hard to locate any research that suggests sitting at your desk for hours on end delivers the same impact.
Reflect and plan. You may also utilize these pauses to continue thinking about other parts of

life and work. When your brain concentrates on different thoughts and concepts, it helps generate solutions.

Socialize and create connections. Entrepreneurs can't operate in a vacuum. It's crucial to engage with other people and cultivate the social element of your life. It builds those vital ties we need in both business and personal life.

If you're struggling to take pauses, I strongly suggest Rest: Why You Get More Done When You Work Less by Alex Soojung-Kim Pang. It will affect the way you work.

6 – Don't Be Afraid to Ask for Help

Getting assistance cleaning the kitchen

We women sometimes are harsh on ourselves, believing the Wonder Woman cape must be in place at all times. For many of us, it takes more than superpowers to ask for assistance or, even better, to delegate with confidence.

Talk to your family. Get them advice on what they'd want to do to reduce your list. Post assignments in a convenient spot. Or, if you are a tech-crazy family, utilize a cloud-based spreadsheet to manage allotted responsibilities. Make space in the budget for service assistance. It's alright to remove something off your plate. If your family can't assist, it can make sense to hire someone to give you a hand. Measure the time it takes for you to accomplish those activities versus the expense. It may be "cheaper" to hire a housecleaner than spend time on it yourself.

Add talent that can help with business-related duties. Find freelancers for projects or part-time assistance to lessen your burden.

Always reward those who aid you. Then, they know you respect their efforts and acknowledge their skill sets. That gratitude is likely to gain you additional aid in the future.

You don't need to carry the world on your shoulders. Let your friends and family know how they can assist you to handle the strain. Even if it's only minding the kids for 20 minutes so you can take a shower or complete a conference call in quiet.

7 - Say "No" to Distractions and Time Suckers More Often.

Entrepreneurs urging themselves to concentrate

As superhero women, we are sometimes afflicted with the inability to say "no" to others.

It may be in our nature to desire to assist. Or, we are concerned someone will think we are disrespectful for turning down a job or cutting a call short. But for excellent time management, we must practice saying "no." Your time has worth, and others will learn to appreciate you establishing limits.

And in exchange, you may gain some much-needed time.

Recognize time suckers. They may get to you over the phone or even via an instant message service. It may even be a customer or an employee.

Make talks short. Or, set an online status to "do not disturb" or "away." Also, there's nothing wrong with not answering the phone or delaying to react to an email. Technology is there for your convenience, not as another distraction.

Assess projects for their time-money value. You don't want to accept assignments that consume important time but don't compensate you for the work.

Remember that you don't need everyone to say "yes" to you all the time. So, don't fall victim to the assumption that people demand it of you.

Time is On Your Side

When it comes to time management, the number one thing to remember is that it's your time. You own it. You determine how you spend it.

Good time management skills help you receive the maximum return for your investment. Improving your business, your health, and your family life.

3: That you are not enough to succeed

No matter how wonderful our life may appear or feel, if there's anything we are always going to suffer from it is the sensation of not being good enough. We could get fantastic marks in school, a full-time job, and have loving friends and long-term relationships yet from time to time the feeling that we're not good enough might come to control our brains. "I'm not good enough for the job", "I'm not attractive", "I'm not very popular" or "I'm not enough for my girlfriend/boyfriend" are just some of the ways that this sensation may show up and have a major influence on how we think, feel and behave.

The sense of not being good enough might drive individuals to acquire what is known as the "impostor syndrome". With this individuals doubt all their successes and persuade themselves that they're phony and going to be discovered at any point. To make things worse, we might also start believing that everyone around us is so much better at what they do.

Social media appears to merely emphasize that everyone else is having a better life than us and potentially prompts us to think"she has a lot better career than me", or "Look at their family, they are great together; that's nothing like ours", "I will never be like him/her". This is certainly something you can connect to.

Our inner critic might be so loud that it can utterly paralyze us. When this occurs, we may tend to embrace it as a realistic picture of reality, with the consequence that we cease doing what we care about. You can certainly recall a moment when you didn't accomplish anything because your "not good enough" thoughts popped up.
If we are interested in growing ourselves and establishing a meaningful life, we need to discover strategies to cope with these ideas before they paralyze us and prevent us from achieving what we value in life.

So what would be an effective approach to coping with that old notion?

Recognize that previous techniques of coping with it don't work

When similar ideas came up in the past what did you attempt to conquer them? Did you attempt suppressing them at all costs as if they were not there? Perhaps uttering things, "get away", or "just stop". You could have attempted to escape them by doing something that makes you feel better, to take your attention away from the discomfort. Binge eating and drinking, using tranquilizers, and watching TV mindlessly are standard methods that we all adopt. Or maybe you attempted to regulate the thoughts? Maybe employing positive thinking, repeating affirmations, stating you are the most wonderful person in the world, all to offset those negative ideas. Another typical method is to avoid circumstances that correspond to such ideas. For example, if you believe you are not good enough to find a relationship, you could avoid meeting new people. Or if you believe you are not competent enough at your work, you can start avoiding specific responsibilities and difficulties that might lead to a promotion.

Just ask yourself: did it truly work? Did those thoughts disappear? Are they no longer a problem? I would suppose that they didn't work for you, else, you wouldn't be reading this essay. Imagine how much vital time you lost in your quest to rid yourself of these sensations. How long did you spend attempting to regulate, suppress or avoid them? What if you had utilized this time to construct a life that had meaning for you? Would things be different now?

Step one is to understand that usual techniques don't work. Once you know that, you may begin to create new talents that work. The alternative actions described here are all backed up by research utilizing a mindfulness-based psychological method called Acceptance and Commitment Therapy (ACT).

Don't battle with them - Accept that they are frequent and normal.

To modify our connection with these persistent ideas, we need to recognize that our brains tend to act automatically and that we have far less control over our minds than we assume. If you want to test this, simply attempt to stop thinking for 30 seconds or so. How did you do? Did you stop thinking? Or did you notice that ideas appeared to come out of nowhere?

To make matters worse, we have what psychologists term “the negativity bias” that makes bad events more noticeable than a favorable ones. You might undoubtedly remember having a very nice day, full of pleasant events but all that was required to destroy it was one poor contact with a work colleague or a message from your spouse fussing about something you missed. That negative encounter lingered with you for a long time. It’s acknowledged today that our brains are programmed this way to help us survive. In our early days as a species, paying attention to the negative was a matter of life and death. Remember it’s your mind attempting to rescue you. And it is a crucial function of the human mind, yet this process may occasionally operate against us.

If we can't control our thoughts and they are virtually automatic, what can we do?

What if, instead of attempting to control, repress and avoid them, you could simply let them be? This is where acceptance comes in. When we accept our emotions, we just allow them to be. We don't fight against them and we don't strive to alter them. Eventually, they will go away. An attitude of acceptance helps us to avoid wasting valuable time attempting to control the uncontrollable and instead frees us to do what we care about despite the unwelcome thoughts and sensations.
When we accept our emotions, we just allow them to be.
We don't fight against them and we don't strive to alter them. Eventually, they will go away.

Don't buy into your ideas

Once we grasp that ideas are automatic and tend to include an element of negative bias, we may start modifying our relationship with them. There is a crucial distinction between having a notion and investing in a thought. We have thoughts all the time, every day. They may be reminders of things we have to accomplish for work, a plan for how to spend the weekend, something to purchase at the grocery or they could be about the world or ourselves. That's pretty simple to grasp, but how can one not buy into a thought? Imagine that your mind is like a store providing a large selection of things. Others of the things you enjoy, some you don't, some are crucial to you as they help you live your life better, some don't contribute much to your life but you still feel convinced to purchase them. Just like entering a store, you don't get to pick what things they sell. You may despise that they have a significant chunk of stuff you don't find helpful or even loathe but it's most probable that you'll simply observe it, accept it, and move on to acquire what you believe is essential. You may choose to interact with the goods you feel are valuable to you.

You may do the same with your ideas. You may have some ideas that you don't like, others you adore, and some that you are ambivalent about. In the same way that you buy things in a store, you may choose which ideas to pay attention to.

So if you notice a thought that you don't like, simply recognize it, stating something like " Ah that's bad thinking" and go on to what is important to you.

Another good method to disconnect from such ideas is by generating space for them. You may accomplish this by stating things like "My mind is suggesting that I'm an idiot" or "My mind is saying that I'm not good enough for the job". By doing this we may establish some space for our ideas and decrease their influence on us. We start noticing that the mind has its concepts that don't rely much on our volition. It's almost like it's coming from someone else. And as when thoughts arrive from other people, we may choose not to become involved with them if we don't find the topic important.

Be more present

Be more conscious, live in the now, practicing meditation. These are common phrases we regularly hear, and with good reason. Usually, when we have bad thinking about ourselves, such ideas tend to be about something in the past. We can't simply stop worrying about them thinking things like "why did I do that?" "Why am I so stupid?". Or they might be about the future when we picture the endless ways things can go wrong for us, ideas like "I'm sure she will leave me, I'm not enough for her" or "I'll mess things up again in tomorrow's presentation".

If we pause to concentrate on what's truly occurring at the time, we would discover that this unpleasant sensation is originating simply from our brains. There's nothing now threatening us. Our imaginations are causing this worry. So it makes sense to cultivate the talent of progressively turning away from what's going inside of our heads to what's happening at the time.

One of the best strategies to bring you back to the present moment is to utilize brief reminders or cues to make your focus wander forth. An excellent one is to enquire from time to time "What is occurring right now?". By doing so you will recognize what's occurring and will gently train your attention to the moment. For example, you may say "I'm having a thought about tomorrow's presentation" "I'm sitting at my desk doing some work" and " I can hear people conversing in the next room".

A closely linked reminder is to pay attention to your surroundings utilizing the "5-4-3-2-1" method. Looking for 5 things you can see, 4 things you can hear, 3 things you can touch, 2 you can smell, and 1 you can taste. That will help you disconnect from your thoughts and will make you connect to what's occurring around you instead of getting lost in a spiral of ideas.

Engaged with what is genuinely essential to you.

Whenever we engage with negative ideas, we lose out on what's genuinely essential to us. The ideas feel so vivid and strong that we might be swept away by them and lose focus on our values and the sort of person we want to be.

Having a clear image of what is significant to us and connecting with it is an excellent strategy to decrease the influence of whatever our brains manufacture. A good example of this would be an athlete preparing for a prestigious competition. It's almost certain that during preparation much doubt would emerge, making the athlete question her abilities. By connecting with the value of "courage" and "skilfulness", this athlete would adjust her conduct and concentrate on how vital is for her to be courageous in the face of difficulties and that she wants to be the sort of person who is constantly seeking for ways to enhance her talents. In the service of a "bigger cause", her own beliefs, she may create room for any ideas that may emerge. If you don't have a clear idea of what your values are, ask yourself basic questions like "What's truly important" and "What do I want to stand for in life?". Or, by thinking that you are holding your 80th birthday celebration and that at this gathering people will make speeches about you. What would you want people to say about you and your qualities? What type of attributes do you most admire? Once you have identified your beliefs, utilize them to guide your behavior in the world. Stop from time to time and merely ask: "Is what I am going to do linked to any of my values?" "Is this the type of person I want to be? Even if we are not athletes we may keep these instances in mind and ask oneself "Am I ready to endure these unpleasant sensations in the cause of something bigger?"

10 Things to Do When You Still Think You're Not Good Enough.

Irrespective of whatever a circumstance requires, are you feeling not good enough, that you're falling short?
If you do, the first thing you need to know is that you are not alone. In truth, we're all in this together.

I truly believe every human reaches this era when life presents tremendously harsh questions. And simply because we cannot answer every unforeseen question, most of us acquire a sense of despondency.
However, these tough moments are crucial for your transition into a stronger and more optimistic person.
Feeling not good enough may make you or destroy you. I'm sure you want to make your

way past those black clouds lurking over you. Are you fired up for the challenge?
Here are 10 things to do when you believe you're not good enough.

1. Stop Comparing and Competing
Everyone is wired differently. But the trouble with most of us is that, in the desire to become like everyone else, we lose our individuality.
With such, we lose an important quality: self-love.
The never-ending comparison with individuals might generate a feeling of worthlessness, particularly now when social media feeds are full of stunning photographs to compare our lives to. However, these nuggets don't reflect the intricacies of life.

One research revealed that "participants who used Facebook most frequently had weaker trait self-esteem, and this was mediated by higher exposure to upward social comparisons on social media. The more you compare, the worse you feel.

Take a minute to observe the beautiful things in your own life, and only compare yourself to who you were yesterday.

2. Recall Your Past Achievements
If you can believe you are not good enough, trust me, you are competent enough to feel proud of yourself. Any happy feeling from your memory book might brighten your thoughts and invigorate you.
Be it the simplest thing, any sense of your prior successes can assist offset the sensation of uselessness.
Switch on your positive reminders. It's the ideal antidote.

3. Deactivate the Thinking Mode for Some Time
Fortunately, this isn't as complicated as it seems. The mind is a strong creature, and in a heartbeat, it may boost or demolish your mood because of the beliefs hidden beneath your sensations.

When you believe you are not good enough, realize it is simply the frequency and quality of ideas that need to change, not you.

Everyone confronts these rough periods when you can't do anything to improve things. The greatest way is to let this period pass without overthinking.

Instead of contemplating and worrying, do something to keep your mind off the unpleasant ideas. It might be exercising, drawing, reading, or conversing with a buddy. Find what works for you.

4. Express the Negativity

Expressing unpleasant feelings is crucial. It is the easiest method to unburden yourself from the anguish of feeling not good enough.

Simply, anytime you feel anything is not right around or within you, speak up! It could demand heroic guts in the beginning. If you don't have someone nearby to speak out, write down your unpleasant sentiments in a notebook. This is another approach to dumping the ideas that are giving you trouble.

5. Choose the Right Person to Share Your Lows

You simply cannot disclose your true unfiltered feelings in front of everyone. This includes a degree of vulnerability that necessitates confidence and safety.

When you are anticipating a shoulder to rest on that is not there, the impacts of feeling worthless may compound and worsen your agony, therefore this decision must be a mindful one.

Make sure you pour out sentiments of your hard moments to one who understands you well. You may not receive the advice you're seeking, but you may gain the fortitude to fight through the bad times if you know you have a support system behind you.

6. Offer an Act of Compassion

Compassion means "to suffer together." Among emotion researchers, it is defined as the feeling that arises when you are confronted with another's suffering and feel motivated to relieve that suffering[3].

Yes, one of the finest methods of resurrecting your higher self is through uplifting others. When you meet the emotional or financial needs of others, not only does it bring a smile to their face, but it also helps you feel pleased. Don't trust me? Try it!

7. Focus on the Process Rather Than the Results
Do you regularly think about the things related to achievement before attaining something?

It is a frequent condition for many individuals in our fast-paced, materialistic environment. We think about the name, fame, and luxury attached to success so much that when we come back to reality, it leads to frustration and impatience. We simply lose focus which adversely affects the execution of the process.

Why? Your mind refuses to persevere because it has tasted triumph in imagining. Then, insecurity seeps in to provoke the thought that you are not good enough.

Wondering what to do? Resist the urge to overthink success by establishing self-control.

8. Work out to Experience Liveliness

Feeling not good enough? Most of the time, a little exercise session is all you need to drive yourself back to life.

Any sort of exercise not only detoxifies your body but also produces joyful hormones in our thoughts. You don't need to go to the gym every time; there are various workouts to assist you to keep on track from home.
A healthy body and mind are the ideal combo to recover from your lows promptly.

9. Stop Fulfilling the Undue Expectations of People
Are you constantly attempting to meet others' expectations of you? Most of us have been doing this for a long time.

If yes, you are digging your own grave. Not only will you lose people, but you'll also lose your personality. If that persists, you won't be able to respect your priorities. It is guaranteed to induce the sensation of uselessness.

Learn to say no to expectations and, instead, pursue your path with the people who accept it.

10. Stop Criticizing Life and Start Appreciating It

Are you gifted with the essential requirements of life required to qualify for happiness—food, clothes, and shelter?

If you are this fortunate, you are ahead of most of the world's population. So, whenever you think you are not good enough, just stop and appreciate your life for all the blessings it bestows on you.

A strong feeling of thankfulness helps you to see the wider picture, and you adjust to tough conditions better.

Final Thoughts:

"All of life is peaks and troughs. Don't let the peaks get too high and the valleys too low." -John Wooden

Look on the bright side! You are one courageous person who has the guts to acknowledge that something isn't quite right.

Not only that, but you are also ready to correct it.
If you are not feeling well enough, it suggests your feeling quotient is operating fine. And that's terrific!

The only problem is the irrepressible negative thoughts that lead you away from optimism. What you need to do is slow down the thought process and gradually resurrect your optimistic self.

Always remember Whenever you feel bad, you need to manage yourself with additional love and care.

4: Afraid of failure and think you have try so many things.

Fear of failing is highly widespread. It's the ultimate loss, leading to confusion, grief, and self-doubt. So would it surprise you to find that most top achievers regard failure as one of their biggest fears?
The difference is that they've learned how to overcome the fear of failure by recognizing and utilizing those sensations - using them to climb even higher.

Maybe your company gained success rapidly and you are now barely holding on, uncertain of where to go next. Maybe your previous relationship went terribly and now you're frightened of allowing anybody in at all. Or maybe you're trapped in an unfulfilling existence because your fear of failure prohibits you from making adjustments.

Overcoming fear of failure entails knowing that it's not about the battle or "failure" itself. It's about how you interpret the failure and treat yourself in its aftermath that eventually creates your result. By adopting an attitude of learning and curiosity, you're able to learn from failure and utilize it to achieve even more in the future.

Fear of failing is highly widespread. It's the ultimate loss, leading to confusion, grief, and self-doubt. So would it surprise you to find that most top achievers regard failure as one of their biggest fears?
The difference is that they've learned how to overcome the fear of failure by recognizing and utilizing those sensations - using them to climb even higher.

Maybe your company gained success rapidly and you are now barely holding on, uncertain of where to go next. Maybe your previous relationship went terribly and now you're frightened of allowing anybody in at all. Or maybe you're trapped in an unfulfilling existence because your fear of failure prohibits you from making adjustments.

Overcoming fear of failure entails knowing that it's not about the battle or "failure" itself. It's about how you interpret the failure and treat yourself in its aftermath that eventually creates your result. By adopting an attitude of learning and curiosity, you're able to learn from failure and utilize it to achieve even more in the future.

FOUR SIGNS YOU HAVE A FEAR OF FAILURE

Learning how to overcome the fear of failure begins with recognizing it. The dread of failure isn't always clear. This dread doesn't emerge the way other acute anxieties, like public speaking or social anxiety, express themselves. You probably won't have sweaty hands and a racing heart from a fear of failing. Instead, you'll observe one – or all – of these four indications.

1. YOU WORRY ABOUT WHAT OTHERS THINK

Humans are social beings, and it's natural to care about what others think — up to a point. But worrying too much about what others say may lead to a paralyzing dread of failure. Whether you're scared people will think less of you, be disappointed in you, or simply not find you very entertaining to be around, overcoming fear of failure always includes appreciating the one opinion that matters: your own.

2. YOU SET LOW EXPECTATIONS FOR YOURSELF

Do you regularly tell folks that you're "not very good" at something or that you don't anticipate you'll be able to succeed? Are you merely "trying it out" without putting forth your whole effort? These are all symptoms that you have a fear of failing. By having modest standards for yourself, you're shielding yourself from criticism — from yourself and others.

3. YOU PROCRASTINATE

Like establishing low expectations, delaying is a means of shielding oneself from failure. If you find yourself creating excuses – whether you don't have time, energy, or the resources you need to fulfill your objectives - it's simply a defensive mechanism against your fear of failing. If you never get started, you can't fail.

4. YOU CAN'T MOVE ON FROM FAILURES

Those with dread of failure yet achieve much in life. The difference between attaining your peak condition and just surviving is in your attitude when you do fail. It's okay to feel sad and disappointed, but if you tend to dwell in these feelings or suffer extended misery, it might be because you're not able to identify the lessons and move on - two fundamental criteria if you are to learn how to overcome the fear of failure.

Now let's discuss how to overcome the fear of failing.

Are you concerned that you are going to fail in business? Relax. Every successful entrepreneur or company owner has gone through such anxieties. The difference is that they understood how to overcome the fear of failure in business.
Fear of failure is unavoidable and you need to conquer your anxieties at whatever cost to achieve in business.

Your concerns will do everything to deter you from taking action and harm your company likewise.

However, it will be impossible to expand your company while you are consumed with the dread of failure.
If you're a small company owner or self-employed, it's crucial to be able to make rapid, solid judgments that balance risk and reward. Knowing you can trust your judgments is frequently important to the success of your company.

While being concerned about failing is fine – and may even help guide you away from undue risk - issues come when our fear of failure takes control. At an extreme, fear of failure may be paralyzing. It may impede innovation, make individuals delay decision-making, and thus lose out on chances.

1:Accept and embrace failure
You simply need to spend five minutes on social media to risk slipping into the trap of believing that failure is something that only occurs to certain individuals. Every day we're inundated on social media with personal and professional achievements tales.

It's crucial to realize that frequently what you're seeing online is carefully edited snippets of people's lives.
The reality is: that everyone fails – often spectacularly.

It might be good to speak to the people around you about instances when they have faced failure. Everyone has a story. Share those humiliating or tough recollections to remind yourself that failing is both common and good.

2:Rewiring how we learn

Now that we know that failure is a part of life, let's look at what can be done to get the most out of our unavoidable blunders.
Simply failing and repeating is useless, so it's vital – and useful – to pause, take a minute, and evaluate.

While it may seem like a difficult endeavor, putting time apart to examine where you went wrong might enable you to convert failure into personal or professional progress.

Set up a system where you ask yourself a series of questions, such as:\sWhat went wrong?
If I got the opportunity again, what might be done better next time?
Is there anything I can gain from this experience?
Is there a chance to educate my team/employees on this experience?
If you find this strategy beneficial, you may even urge your staff to adopt the same tactics. Together you may start viewing failure as an opportunity for shared learning.

3:Adopt a Beginner Mindset
Contrary to the name, a 'beginner's mindset is a tool that can be utilized by everyone - from professionals to novices.

The trick here is to approach a task or a profession as if you are a newbie, regardless of your expertise. This may make it easier to let go of the expectations we set on ourselves that might lead to the dread of failure.

In business, this strategy not only helps liberate us from fear of failure but is shown to help drive creativity and boost our capacity to learn new things. By being open-minded and listening to others without pre-judgment, we are more receptive to new ideas and may discover innovative solutions to issues.

This is a strategy that has origins well outside the western commercial sector. In Zen Buddhism, Shoshin is the practice of having a 'beginner's mind' and refers to having an attitude of openness and interest while learning a topic, even when studying at an advanced level.

Thankfully it doesn't take years of meditation to start to transform your mentality. You may start to modify how you tackle new issues now.

4:Manage your expectations

Too frequently fear of failure might arise from unreasonable or poorly defined expectations.

Sometimes, without even knowing it, we regard failure or achievement as an all-or-nothing consequence. So, it might be good to moderate our expectations and reframe what failure looks like.

For example, John is anxious to take the leap and start his own company but finds himself immobilized by fear of failure. John takes the time to explore his expectations surrounding failure. He had previously anticipated the firm to become profitable within a few months. This self-imposed deadline was keeping him from ever launching the firm at all.

By beginning modestly and controlling his expectations, John can take the initial steps toward becoming self-employed.

Being honest with yourself and your company about what your expectations are, may assist in better managing risk without being driven by fear.

5:You don't have to go it alone
In certain circumstances, fear of failure may be related to other mental health issues such as anxiety or depression. Exploring and treating mental health disorders such as these via the

aid of medical specialists (such as your GP, a therapist, or a psychiatrist) may be useful.
Contacting your GP to discuss any mental health problems may be a fantastic starting step.

6:Be hopeful.
You need to be positive about the future and anticipate the best. It will empower you and excite you to take strong measures to succeed in business.
Otherwise, your anxieties will overwhelm you and fill you with bad energy which will undoubtedly lead you to failure.
The easiest strategy to overcome failure in business fears is to remain enthusiastic about the future and your company.
It will allow you to break your boundaries and take action that leads to success.
Optimistic folks see the world as full of possibility. You cannot find them whining about anything. This is the reason so many individuals aspire to become optimistic people.
But they never obtain the correct knowledge which may allow them to become one.

You will always find optimists pursuing their aspirations and huge objectives in life. They are successful in all they do.

If you want to become an optimist, you are in the proper location.

Here are 7 Best Ways To Become An Optimistic Person.

A. Think as large as possible.

Optimistic folks think big. When I say huge, it means as big as possible. They establish high attainable targets. It's hard for them to think tiny.

They establish high expectations from life.

You will never find an optimistic individual talking about tiny ideas or aspirations.

You need to start thinking as large as possible to become an optimist.

B. Focus on solutions.

When the entire world is confronting the issue and moaning about it, Optimistic individuals are seeking solutions.

Optimistic individuals are the ones who are changing the world for the better.

They never complain about anything. Because they are problem solvers.
You need to start concentrating on solutions to become an optimistic person.

C. Surround yourself with winners.
Surround yourself with individuals who will raise you. They will assist you to dream big and accomplishing great things in life.
You cannot succeed by remaining with tiny minds.
You need to hang around with winners and someday you will become one.
You need a mentality that winners have, then you can win in life as well.
D. Keep your eyes on the objectives.
Optimistic individuals never feel terrified in tough situations. No matter how harsh the scenario is presented, they will maintain their eyes on the objectives.

Most individuals quit in tough circumstances and this is what divides optimistic people from typical people (pessimists). (pessimists).
When things get challenging, optimistic individuals boost their game and play harder.

You need to maintain your sights on objectives amid tough circumstances to become an optimistic person.

E. Believe.

Optimistic persons are a believer. They think that everything is possible. It gets them revved up with good energy.

They extend their bounds and it makes them assume that there are no restrictions in life.

It allows them to realize their maximum potential and extend it even further.

Start believing and you will be a positive person in life.

F. Never listen to tiny minds.

Optimistic individuals never listen to tiny thoughts. People will attempt to persuade you that you are dreaming too large or it's impossible to reach your objective.

Never even trust those folks who attempt to tear you down.

Listen to those individuals who have attained the achievement you seek in life.

G. Take charge of your life.

Optimistic individuals are the controller of their life. They are not the victim of their circumstances. However, they take command of their life.

You cannot find any optimistic individual playing the blame game of excuses.

You need to take charge of your life to become an optimistic person.

Conclusion

Successful individuals are optimistic people. If you want to become successful in life, you need to become a positive person.

Start thinking as large as feasible for you and attempt to concentrate on solutions.

You must surround yourself with winners who lift you and believe to accomplish success in life.

Make sure you maintain your eyes on the objectives and discover answers whenever a difficulty emerges along the route.

Stay away from tiny brains and never listen to them. And don't let anything dictate your life.

7:Learn more than other folks.

Every successful entrepreneur, CEO's and business professional read at least 1 book every month. They are hooked to learning new things

daily. Learning and developing are key to success in business.
It will allow you to obtain more skills and information that leads to success.

Chapter:3

Behaviours to adopt (millionaires behaviours)

Humans are creatures of habit, and a lot of us creatures are in debt.
What habits got us there? How did we fall into a life of anxiety over credit card bills, paying off loans, and avoiding calls from debt collectors?

It was largely a matter of habit. Thanks to research by Thomas C. Corley, we know what those habits are.

Corley is a financial planner and author who spent five years studying millionaires. He wasn't out to discover the investment strategies they shared. He wanted to find out general stuff, like how they lived, what TV shows they watched, and what **they ate.** Those habits can be as crucial to building wealth as investing in the right stocks.

Corley interviewed 233 people who make at least $160,000 a year in gross income and have

$3.2 million in net assets. The majority of them, 177 in all, were self-made millionaires.

Those creatures have the right habits to acquire wealth, but what about the other side of that coin? Do low-income people share lifestyle habits?

Corley interviewed 128 Americans who make $35,000 or less in gross annual income and have $5,000 or less in liquid assets.

The research showed wealthy people indeed have what Corley calls "rich habits."

Among them are they don't watch more than one hour of TV daily, they count calories, and – at the risk of sounding like your mother – they floss their teeth.

You might not see the connection between good oral hygiene and a healthy bank account, but flossing takes discipline. If you don't have that, it's easy to fall into what Corley calls "poverty habits."

If you want to get rich, here are seven "poverty habits" that handcuff people to a life of low income.

1. Plan and set goals.

As is so often the case, we may know what to do, but seldom do we do it.
So what about you? Are you regularly setting goals and reviewing them? Are you walking the talk? Remember, to know and not do is to not know at all.

The information in this article may sound "old-hat" to a lot of readers, but the very same people who are yawning probably aren't walking the talk.

Four of the most dangerous words in the English language are "I already know that".

You may know it intellectually, but if you aren't already setting and achieving goals habitually, then it would pay for you to follow closely below so that you can begin using this valuable tool to its fullest potential.

Step One: Begin The Goal Setting Process In January.
We begin our annual goal-setting cycle in the weeks surrounding New Year's Day. Why? Because it's virtually impossible to forget or avoid this annual holiday event.

The New Year is a natural time to reflect on achievements from the prior year and start thinking about what we want to achieve in the coming year. In short, it's a perfect time to begin a goal-setting cycle.

Your first task is to review your written goals from the prior year and compare them to your actual results.

"No one can cheat you out of ultimate success but yourself."
– Ralph Waldo Emerson

Inevitably, your results will exceed expectations in some areas, and disappoint in others. The critical point here is to not judge yourself because you're not your results.

Instead, I suggest positive reinforcement by rewarding yourself for all that you did achieve in the prior year. Take the time to celebrate your wins because you deserve it. Also note areas where you came up short, as that is honoring reality.

What are your results telling you? If you came up short on a goal, then what was the cause?

After all, if you said you wanted a goal, but didn't achieve it, then there is a learning opportunity.
Did something change?
Did other goals take a higher priority
Did obstacles get in your way?
Maybe you're just not committed to that goal and should drop it or change it.
You don't get to be right or wrong during the review process, as that won't serve you well. There's no value in belittling yourself for missing a goal because that will just take away from honoring your successes.

The purpose is simply to get clear on what worked in the prior year and what didn't. Just notice the facts and make conscious of what happened, but don't judge yourself.

"When defeat comes, accept it as a signal that your plans are not sound, rebuild those plans, and set sail once more toward your coveted goal."
– Napolean Hill

Where did you meet with success, and where did you come up short? Your objective is to learn from experience and improve your goal setting for next year based on what you discover.
You're creating an active feedback loop so you can correct and adjust your goals every year to get what you want out of life.

This correct and adjusted process works much like rocket guidance systems. When a rocket is launched to a faraway destination, it's traveling off course more than 80 percent of the time. Yet, the same rocket will hit its target with pinpoint accuracy. The key is correcting and adjusting.

The rocket knows its goal and is constantly correcting its trajectory during the flight until it arrives at the destination. You can do the same thing by reviewing your goals each year and learning from your successes, as well as your failures.

Step Two: Prepare Financial Statements.
The next step during the annual review process is to compose a "quick and dirty" income statement and balance sheet.
This task is particularly easy around the turn of the year because annual tax statements must be prepared showing your assets, income, and spending.

When you prepare these statements you are treating your finances with the professionalism of a business. You're respecting your money.

I also suggest plotting your net worth and residual income on a chart so you can track your progress toward your goal of financial freedom. This is very important if you're working toward the goal of financial independence or retirement security.

“The person who makes a success of living is the one who sees his goal steadily and aims for it unswervingly. That is dedication.”
– Cecil B. DeMille

Once you've updated your financial statements and reviewed your past goals, you're then complete with the feedback loop portion of the process.

You now have a solid foundation on which to build your new goals. You have a current snapshot of your financial picture, and you understand what worked from the prior year, what didn't, and why.

Step Three: Ask The Right Questions.

The next step in your annual goal-setting process is to decide what you want to create with your life moving forward by asking yourself some questions:

What do I want this year?

What will it take for this year to rate as a 10 on a scale of 1 to 10?

If failure was not a possibility because I'm guaranteed success, then what would I do? How would I play the game of life differently?

What values do I hold dear that I would like to honor in the New Year?

What's frustrating or dissatisfying about my life, and how would I like to change it?

If I graded the various parts of my life (relationships, business, money, health, recreation, etc.) on a 1 to 10 scale, what grade would each receive, and what do I want to do this year to create the grades I want?

What objectives would make the biggest, most profound difference in my life?

Step Four: Compile And Prioritize Your List Of Goals

After I've answered these questions, I get together with my wife to create a combined goal sheet for the family. She follows a similar process independent of me and creates her agenda.

We then compare lists and create a combined family agenda for the year that's broken into two categories: the first list has business and financial goals, and the second list has our personal and family life goals.
It's important to note that we don't just add the lists up to create one summation list. Instead, we negotiate the goals knowing that we must focus to succeed.
Less is more, and this is critical to note. More goals don't equal more success, but more focus on just a few goals that make the biggest difference will equal more success.

We compare our goals to the "10 Keys To A Winning Goal" checklist found in Step Two of the Seven Steps to Seven Figures course that this article is excerpted from, and we put on the back burner those goals that don't make it to the top.

After years of practice, we have learned to enjoy greater balance and happiness by focusing on just a few critical goals and achieving them, rather than setting ourselves up for disappointment by getting spread too thin with too many goals.

What amazes me about this process is how powerful it is while being deceptively simple.
It never fails to redirect our thinking.

It creates clarity and cohesive focus for both of us to operate as a team and helps us create a more satisfying and fulfilling life for our family.

It redirects our lives and keeps us from drifting aimlessly or living day to day.

Step Five: Get Into Action To Achieve Your Goals.
Once you've set your goals, you now have a whole year to achieve them. But how are you going to do that? What is your next step? My suggestion is to divide and conquer.
Keep things simple by picking from the list only those goals that are the most exciting and juiciest of all, so you can focus your limited time and energy resources on them.

What's your top priority for the year? What's the most time-sensitive or immediately compelling goal on your list?

"The big secret in life is that there is no big secret. Whatever your goal, you can get there if you're willing to work."
– Oprah Winfrey.

Once your goals are prioritized, then you can pick either of the two strategies from below to begin executing your plan of action.
I offer two different strategies because each is appropriate for different situations, depending on conditions. Certain goals and personality types work best with one or the other approach. Which of the following approaches is best will depend on your style and the particular goal you are pursuing.

Next Step Approach: This is a forward-looking approach where you just pick the next step to achieve your goal, complete it before figuring out the next step, and so on until your goal is realized. You don't worry about the big picture with all the planning issues (which might bog you down because too much is unknown, or the whole process is too big to grasp) (which might bog you down because too much is unknown, or the whole process is too big to grasp). Instead, you just determine whatever the logical next step is, and trust it'll take you to the next step until the path becomes clear. You're like the rocket that's correcting and adjusting its flight path. This also helps you avoid the "get ready to get ready" syndrome so that you can get started right now and not get stuck in procrastination excuses.

Reverse Engineering: This approach requires you to start with the whole plan in mind from the beginning by reverse engineering it into smaller tasks to complete. You then further subdivide the tasks into additional actionable steps, while continuing to break them down until you have daily actions that will take you to your goal when completed. The advantage of this process is it breaks big tasks down into digestible bite-size chunks, making the whole process very easy to grasp. It's most effective for analytical personality types or situations where the entire path to the goal can be understood and mapped out in advance.

Both of these approaches help you succeed by reducing the intimidation and confusion that is sometimes associated with larger goals that take us into unfamiliar territory. They reduce your fear factor by transforming goals that are too large to grasp into actionable items that you can easily execute.

Each strategy answers the question, "where do I start?" and "where do I go next?" so that you don't get stuck in procrastination.

Step Six: Persist Until You Achieve Your Goal

"Let me tell you the secret that has led me to my goal. My strength lies solely in my tenacity."
– Louis Pasteur.

Once you have picked your goal and developed your plan to achieve the goal, then the rest of the game is simply a matter of getting started and not stopping until you reach it.

Every time you complete an action step, you're one small step closer to your big goal.

Just keep on correcting and adjusting until you get there with rocket-like accuracy.

Enough said?

Step Seven: Maintain Focus By Reviewing Goals Regularly.

Finally, the last part of this annual cycle is you must create a habit of refreshing your goals throughout the year. This means you must review them regularly and rewrite them as necessary.

The purpose of this step is to maintain your focus throughout the year as life's clutter attempts to distract you from what's important.

By reviewing your goals regularly, you're counteracting all the forces outside of your control designed to sideline your plans.

Some people like to post them on their walls, keep a copy on their desk, or post them on their Day Timer or smartphone. Whatever is convenient and will remind you regularly about your goals so that you maintain a front-of-the-mind awareness is what's important.

"It **matters not what goal you seek**

Its secret here reposes:\sYou've got to dig from week to week\sTo get Results or Roses."
– Edgar Guest

In summary, the seven-step process you just learned is designed to do one thing: make goal setting a habit. You must habitually create and refresh your goals to gain all the value from this incredibly effective tool.
By following a habitual goal-setting process, you'll become part of the 3 percent that outperforms the other 83 percent by a factor of 10 to 1. You'll also put yourself firmly on the road to retiring early and wealthy.
It truly works.

Goal Setting System Key Points

There are three major points you should take from this.

1. Practicing goal setting and reviewing your goals is necessary to live the greatest version of yourself in this lifetime. Not using goal-setting technology to the best of your ability is simply

wasteful. It's the equivalent of flushing opportunity down the toilet.

"You must have long-range goals to keep you from being frustrated by short-range failures."
– Charles C. Noble

2. Goal setting engages your mind in five different ways to achieve your goals. This gives you a distinct competitive advantage over others who don't regularly set and review their goals. This competitive advantage can make the difference between retiring early and being wealthy, or living a life of financial mediocrity.

3. The most effective way to get all the value out of goal setting available is to make it a habit. Set your goals at least annually, and review them at least monthly. Build a regular cycle out of the process so that it becomes an integral part of your life. If you set goals randomly or irregularly, then you will get random and irregular results. If you set and review your goals regularly, you will move them to the forefront of your mental awareness, which will create more consistently profitable results.

The bottom line is if you want to retire early and be wealthy, then regular goal setting must become an integral part of your life practice. Financial coaching is a great tool to add accountability, support, and additional insight to not only setting goals but also following through long enough to achieve them.

2. Don't overspend.

The quickest and surest approach to riches is to save money and invest it. It's like planting an acorn and witnessing it grow into a tree. The issue for millions of Americans is obtaining an acorn to plant.

A 2018 Federal Reserve poll found that four in 10 Americans would not be able to cover an unexpected $400 expense much less an emergency fund. The U.S. Bureau of Labor Statistics estimated it at 6 percent, the lowest level since the 2008 financial crisis.

If you barely make enough money to pay your bills and can't save, the obvious option is to produce more money. That brings us to the second poverty habit.

Financial stability comes from following the foundations of personal finance, like setting a budget, but there's also an emotional role in attitudes and decision-making around money. One classic financial concern, overspending, may be overcome with a combination of practical measures and emotional awareness.

"People need to deal with the psychological element of the money as well as the economic and financial side," says Elizabeth Dunn, professor at the University of British Columbia and chief scientific officer of Happy Money. "People typically have a lot of anxiety and baggage regarding money. Before we start talking about interest rates, let's deal with all of the attitudes and anxiety, and challenges that may be spinning around.

Financial stability comes from following the foundations of personal finance, like setting a budget, but there's also an emotional role in attitudes and decision-making around money. One classic financial concern, overspending, may be overcome with a combination of practical measures and emotional awareness.

Live Frugally Without Browsing Cheap\sWoman looking for clothes at a boutique store.

"People need to deal with the psychological element of the money as well as the economic and financial side," says Elizabeth Dunn, professor at the University of British Columbia and chief scientific officer of Happy Money.

"People typically have a lot of anxiety and baggage regarding money. Before we start talking about interest rates, let's deal with all of the attitudes and anxiety and challenges that may be spinning around."

Overspending may be defined as spending beyond one's means, possibly due to a sudden occurrence, such as a job loss, or a gradual development of financial behaviors. According to a recent Federal Reserve research, more than one-fourth of respondents questioned in 2020 had one or more bills that they were unable to pay in full that month or were one $400 financial setback away from being unable to pay them.

Overspending may also take different forms across families and lifestyles.

"I think of overspending as being about not just spending more than your means but where those causes of bad spending decisions are creeping in," Dunn says. "It's those sorts of purchases that aren't giving a lot in the way of happiness."

Why We Overspend

While every individual's spending habits are unique to his or her circumstances, Shari Greco Reiches, co-founder, partner, and chief visionary officer at Rappaport Reiches Capital Management in Illinois, says a few similar variables tend to be responsible for overspending.

Lifestyle creep, for example, arises when individuals slowly raise their consumption over time and often accounts for unintentional overspending. Individuals who lack a decision-making process for acquiring products could also find it tough to limit their spending.

You continuously expect the next rung is going to make you happy, and if you don't catch it early it might be a steep fall," Greco Reiches says. "The persons who prefer to overspend have no choice process, and a budget is the first step with that."

Media, advertisements, and cultural pressure may all lead to overspending. Marketing strategies strive to create an impression of scarcity for consumers using expressions like "almost sold out" or "two tickets remaining" when completing online purchases. Emails from preferred businesses may give customers the illusion that they are saving money by taking advantage of a deal, and roadside billboards could drive them to make hurried purchases.

Greco Reiches thinks cultural pressures to enjoy dinners out and excursions with family and friends may be heightened for younger persons, who observe others enjoying similar activities on social media platforms like Instagram.
"People believe spending makes you happy," Greco Reiches adds. "But for many folks, it's these ideas of being true to yourself that make you happy.

7 Ways to Rein in Overspending

Having a plan for limiting your expenses is crucial all year long. But when you think about what happens to your checkbook over the

Christmas season, you may find that now is a great opportunity to sort out overspending.

Here are seven techniques to start gaining a hold on it today:

1. Get to know your spending triggers.
It's easy to spend money without thinking about it; but if you want to save money instead, it can be useful to also take a closer look at the "why" behind your spending behaviors.

Several elements may affect what you buy or don't purchase and whether you spend a lot of money or a little.
Some of the objects that could act as spending triggers include:

Your attitude and mindset (i.e. feeling agitated or apprehensive and wanting to spend money to blow off steam) (i.e. feeling stressed or anxious and wanting to spend money to let off steam)
Peer pressure from friends or family (FOMO, anyone?)

Time of day and the weather Environmental variables that drive impulsive purchases, such as the checkout wait at the grocery store.

A good technique to get to know your spending triggers is to keep a spending notebook.

In this diary, you record each of your shopping excursions, whether in-person or online, including what you bought, how much you spent, the time of day, and your thoughts both before and after making the purchase.

Keeping a spending notebook could help you learn control over spending money and lessen how often you give in to the desire to buy on impulse.

A spending notebook may also help you get in the habit of tracking what you spend money on often and make it easier to maintain a budget. A smart approach to monitoring spending automatically is by utilizing budgeting software or signing in to online banking each day to see what you've spent.

2. Clear up your inbox.

One of the easiest methods to limit the amount of money you spend so you may save money is by minimizing the emails that touch your inbox.

For example, you may have signed up to get emails about the newest specials and deals from your favorite businesses. But it merely maintains the desire to spend a lot of money on products you don't need, just because they're on sale or the retailer is giving a digital voucher.

This may be particularly problematic coming up to Black Friday and the commencement of the holiday season when merchants are seeking to catch shoppers' attention with special bargains and offers. Unsubscribing from merchant emails is a simple and efficient technique to stave off impulsive purchases right now. Out of sight is out of memory.

You may go a step further and ask shops to remove you from their mailing lists if you often get catalogs or coupons in the mail. If you'd prefer not to be overwhelmed with credit card offers, you can also opt out of getting them so you're not enticed to create a new credit card account you don't need.

3. Don't save credit card data online.

A credit card may make buying products online simple, plus you might earn some significant points on your transactions in the process.

While you could look at it as a means to save money, it might lead you into spending money you didn't want to if you're charging stuff and not keeping track of the total.

This is a personal financial blunder that's simple to make if you're keeping your credit card credentials online via a digital wallet app or at the checkout for your favorite retailers. When you don't have to key in your card information, it's a lot simpler to fill up your basket, click, and make a buy without being careful about what you're spending.

Taking your credit card (or debit card) data out of online checkouts and digital wallet applications means you have to slow down before making purchases online. When you have to get your card out of your wallet and key in the digits, that gives you time to think about the purchase and determine whether it's the actual money you want to spend.

4. Consider being cash-only for a month.
Credit cards are handy – and receiving miles, points, or cash back on purchases is a great reward. But it's conceivable that you may get overly reliant on credit cards for spending money and wind up with a mound of debt. When your card has a high-interest rate, holding a debt may make purchases that much more costly.

If you don't want to discontinue using your credit card entirely, try taking a brief vacation from using it for one month. During that month, commit to spending money using your debit card, cheques, or cash instead.

After the money, examine your purchases and budget to see how much you spent. Then, compare it to a normal month of spending using your credit card. (You may use a prior credit card statement for this portion.)

If you spent less during the month when you weren't using your credit card, it might be an encouragement to keep with the practice and go cash-only for the long run. And even if you didn't save a lot of money, you may at least discover that you don't have to need a credit card to make purchases.

5. Impose a 48-hour rule on new purchases.

Have you ever made an impulsive purchase only to regret it later?

It's a terrible place to be in, particularly if you can't return the item and get your money back. But there is a technique to prevent impulsive purchases in the future and save money.

Imposing a 48-hour limit on new purchases might give you time to consider a purchase to determine whether it's something on which you want to spend your money. If you conclude after the 48 hours is over that it's something you need, then go ahead and buy it.

When putting a 48-hour rule on new purchases, consider providing some criteria. For example, you may specify a financial value that would activate the rule, such as $50 or $100. That way, you're not having to go through a waiting period for every transaction.

For bigger items, you might wait much longer. If you want to purchase anything that's above $500, for example, you may wait a week or even a month. The more time you allow yourself to consider a purchase, the more chance you have to determine whether you want to spend the money.

6. Try a longer spending fast

Spending fast, often called a spending diet, might help you speed up your attempts to save money. The premise behind spending fast is that you promise not to spend money, beyond fundamental living expenditures, for a particular length of time.

You may complete a no-spend challenge for a week, a month — even a whole year. During this period you would spend money on things like rent, utilities, and basic food items at the grocery store. But you cut off useless luxuries like shopping, leisure, vacation, and takeaway dinners.

Spending fast might help you kickstart your savings and offer you insight into where you've been wasting money. It may also help you become in sync with what defines a "want" and a "need" in your budget. The money you don't spend is money you can use to pay off debt or contribute to your emergency savings reserve.

Trying a spending diet might also assist you in blowing your budgets throughout the Christmas season. A no-spend November, for example, maybe a fantastic strategy to avoid the temptation to overpay or make impulsive purchases while stores are rolling out the Black Friday and Christmas specials.

7. Get friends and family on board
Your friends and family might be some of your largest spending triggers if they push you to spend money foolishly. For example, being asked out to interact with friends may entail spending money on dinner, beverages, or other entertainment for which you didn't budget.

If you are serious about avoiding overspending, then let your friends and family know that you're making an effort to save money instead. Rather than going along with pricey activities, propose alternate methods to spend time together that don't need you to spend a lot of money or any money at all.

Your friends and family may not alter their spending habits, but it's still vital to let them know that you're changing yours. That might make saying no to things you'd prefer not to spend money on simpler so you can expand your savings over the long run.

3. Create multiple streams of incomes.

A 2019 U.S. Census Bureau survey indicated that just 8.8 percent of women and 8.0 percent of males had two or more jobs.

Corley observed that 65 percent of affluent persons have at least three separate sources of income established before achieving their first $1 million.

"Poor folks have one revenue stream," he wrote. "Their eggs are all in one basket."

So, if you lose your work, you run into a medical emergency or you get behind paying bills, you're one source of income isn't going to be enough to bail you out.
Building several sources of income is no longer a luxury, it has become a necessity. If the high rate of unemployment and growing job losses have taught us anything, it is that nobody's job is secure. Unfortunately for most individuals, their sole source of money comes from their

employment, which may be a perilous way to live. Some couples may be luckier and have a spouse bringing in money each month, but they are still reliant on work for their existence. Because of the financial dangers connected with depending on work for all of your incoming cash, it is vital to consider having at least one alternative source of income. The list below discusses a few reasons why having various sources of money flowing in is significant and how this additional revenue might be utilized.

Here are seven basic reasons why creating various revenue sources is so vital. Each item described below is an illustration of how other income streams may be leveraged to reduce the danger of living on a single income.

- Rising Health Care Costs Whether you are in favor of the health care reform or not, chances are you are feeling the sting of increasing health care expenditures. Adding income sources may go a long way in paying for things like rising prescription expenses and unexpected medical bills.

- Unemployment How safe is your job? Let's face it, no job is truly ever secure, particularly in a harsh recession. Having extra sources of income may help you cope with a job loss far better than being caught off guard. Even if your other sources of income couldn't cover all of your monthly bills, it might still give you time to work things out.
- Paying for College How much are you saving for your kid's college? Instead of putting your retirement in danger by saving up for your child's secondary school, why not build an alternate income stream to assist out? Having various sources of income flowing in cash every month might assist lessen the stress of paying for education.
- Living Within Your Means To acquire actual wealth, you must be able to live within your means. If it is difficult to limit your expenditure anymore, or you simply don't want to sacrifice any more–create a new source of money. There are only two ways to live within

your means — either spend less or produce more money.

- Pay Cash for Purchases How many times have you been able to pay cash for a vehicle or could pay for a significant home improvement job without taking out a loan? A second or third income source might be utilized to save for these sorts of purchases so you don't have to take out a loan and pay any interest. What a concept—pay less interest and retain more of your money!
- Build a New Income Stream What better approach to spend your spare revenue than utilizing it to build another income stream? If you don't need it to live, then why not utilize your additional money to your advantage to improve your monthly cash flow and become financially independent?
- Pay Down Debt Paying off your house, automobile, or credit cards is a wonderful use for an additional income stream. If you can avoid paying loads of interest on a loan by making additional payments on

current debt, then you might be on your road to financial independence.

Diversified Income Sources Any competent stock broker will advise their clients the number one rule as an investor is to construct a diverse portfolio to decrease risk. If you would diversify your assets, why wouldn't you do the same with your income streams? Creating several revenue streams helps a person to diversify the many cash flow sources that are pouring in. In the case one dries up, then there are other sources of income to mitigate the loss.

Build a Holiday Fund This is something my wife and I recently did when I earned some additional freelancing cash. Instead of wondering about how we would pay for all the additional holiday spending this year, we simply earmarked this other revenue stream to be utilized for the holidays.

Take Control of Income When was the last time you received a raise at work?

Even if you have gotten one in the last year, there is no assurance you will be receiving one next year, given the way the economy is acting. Do yourself a favor and take charge of your money by developing numerous sources of

income. That way you have the authority to offer yourself a raise whenever you choose!
There is no mystical limit as to the number of supplementary revenue streams you should generate. Just as long as the time you spend maintaining them doesn't become too onerous and they provide positive cash flow. There are lots of crucial advantages to developing numerous income streams to lessen the chance of having your primary source of income unexpectedly dry up. Even if your other sources of income cannot match your monthly needs, they may at least assist minimize the shock of a job loss or other unexpected expense. If you are fortunate, these revenue sources might do more than merely boost your income and assist fatten up your savings accounts.

4. Read and educate yourself.

Wealthy folks not only work two jobs, but they also make time to read. But they're not reading Stephen King or Danielle Steel.
They read educational and self-improvement literature. Corley observed that just 8 percent of low income read educational or self-improvement books.

"Success demands progress, he stated. "That progress comes from reading and educating oneself regularly."
Generally speaking, you can't get wealthy solely by reading books. But, reading does play a catalytic function in your road to getting affluent. A majority of successful and affluent individuals do share reading as a common attribute. Reading helps you to learn from others' triumphs, and obtain success quicker.
Does Reading Books Make You Smarter?
While you are currently looking at how reading may make you affluent, you undoubtedly question if reading books makes you smarter overall as well. The answer is "yes" since studies

have proved that the stimulation reading delivers to your brain boosts brain processes and makes you smarter.

Interestingly, it is also commonly acknowledged that self-made millionaires are brilliant individuals. One may conclude that if you can grow smarter, your chances of being affluent are higher.

Thus, reading may make you smarter and wealthier — two very strong reasons to look at the reading habits of "self-made" affluent individuals! Most of the books that they've read, will not only aid you to become money but also grow wiser overall.

Do You Make More Money When You Start Reading Books?

Making money and being affluent always begins with an idea.

Reading books boosts knowledge and helps you to learn from others' experiences. It offers your brain the essential facts and resources to initially generate thoughts on how to earn money. Furthermore, reading also helps you to put these concepts into practice and learn to make sensible judgments.

As Robert Kiyosaki, the author of “Rich Dad, Poor Dad, and entrepreneur puts it: “Money is only an idea... If you want money in your hands, then put an idea in your head.“

Napoleon Hill, the author of “Think and Grow Rich’ famously observed that “all successes, all acquired wealth have their starting in an idea.”
To create money and to get wealthy you must first have thoughts in your brain on how to make money. And the more knowledge and concepts are stored in your brain, the more ideas you will be able to develop. It is not for no cause that reading is considered to make you more creative!
One of the simplest methods to add knowledge to your brain is via reading. When your brain retains information and conceptualizes concepts it doesn’t discriminate between your real-life experiences and those you’ve read about.
So, reading the correct books regularly enough can stimulate your brain to supply you with fresh and original ideas to generate more money.

However, the reason why we provide a "conditional yes" is that you will only generate money after you've chosen to implement your money-making ideas that have come from your reading.

Reading Habits of the Wealthy

According to a study done by Tom Corley, the author of "Rich Habits: The Daily Success Habits of Affluent Individuals," both rich people and poor people may practice reading regularly, but not all become wealthy.

However, if you get into the habit of reading numerous self-improvement books, like most financially successful people, your chances of becoming wealthy are significantly greater than individuals who read solely for amusement.

Several additional studies have indicated that business professionals who are in the habit of reading at least seven business books a year, earn 2.3 times more than business people who only read one business book each year.

From this research, it can be determined that the habit of the rich to read self-improvement and business books is a habit to pursue.

The reading habits of the rich may be stated as follows:

Read regularly.
Read whenever you have the time for it.
Read self-improvement books.
Read business books.
For pleasure, read poetry and well-written books with compelling stories (to strengthen your self-evaluation and critical thinking abilities) (to enhance your self-evaluation and critical thinking skills).
How Many Books Should You Read to Become Successful?
You need to read at least 2 books a month to become successful. However, the quantity of books alone does not ensure success. The quality and the sort of books you study along with your capacity to put the learnings into practice play an equally significant part to reach success.

The precise quantity of books one needs to read to become successful might vary from one individual to another. However, one may look at how many books affluent individuals read.

According to a study, the typical affluent person always keeps in the habit of reading to develop and learn. The overall number of books such a person has read is not as essential as the frequency that books are read — the total number of books is continuously shifting from time to time.

According to research done by Thomas Corley in his book "The Rich Habits" (which by the way you should certainly read!), Thomas reports that 85 percent of self-made millionaires read two or more books every month.

Warren Buffett was once asked what his secret to success was. He said: "Read 500 pages per day. That's how knowledge works. It adds up, like compound interest."

Bill Gates reads more than 50 books every year — at least 1 book per week.

Mark Cuban reads more than 3 hours every day, while millionaire Charlie Munger was quoted: "In my entire life, I have met no sensible individuals (across a large subject matter area) who didn't read all the time."

What Type of Books Should You Read to Become Rich?

To establish what sort of books you should read to get rich, we've looked at what the affluent read. According to a study done by Thomas Corley say 85 percent of affluent individuals read two or more self-improvement, education, and career-related books every month;94 percent of them read news and media; and the books they read are mostly non-fiction, such as biographies and self-help books.

Businesspeople who are reading poetry when they read for pleasure, unknowingly develop their self-reflection talent — a quality most affluent people have.

Self-reflection is the practice of intentionally recollecting prior activities to reflect on your own emotions, ideas, behaviors, and choices. You may then analyze if you have done things efficiently in the past or have to move to better money-making strategies in the future.

To recall facts, you have to engage your autobiographical memory. Reading poetry awakens your memories. This is because poetry is often crafted in such a manner that it entices you to remember personal memories.

So, aside from all the non-fiction, you have to read to become wealthy, read poetry regularly, practice self-reflection, and grow richer!

Correlation Between Reading Books, Critical Thinking and Getting Rich.

To be a great businessman and get affluent, you have to be able to think critically. Well-written books encourage your brain to think in sequences and connect cause and effect. This is in theory the cornerstone of critical thinking.
The more you read, the more your brain adjusts to this mode of thinking, and the more ideas you develop to earn more money. The "recipe" is simple:
Read well-written literature.
Your brain learns to think in sequences.
Your brain learns to think critically about cause and consequence.
You get into the habit of thinking critically in real life about your money-making ideas.

You make practical judgments and grow affluent!

5. Avoid toxic relationships.

Psychology has a big part in wealth building. It may seem clichéd, but a Can-Do mentality is a requirement. It's hard to keep one if you socialize with Can't-Do folks. Corley observed that just 4 percent of low-income persons associate with "success-minded" people. Most of us have encountered a toxic connection at some time in our life whether through personal interactions (friends, family members) or professional (coworkers, etc.) or via an intimate relationship.

Most of us have encountered a toxic connection at some time in our life whether through personal interactions (friends, family members) or professional (coworkers, etc.) or via an intimate relationship.

There are those individuals who are also naysayers, who attempt to hinder you from enjoying the life you desire. The word naysayers are how I refer to the individual and society factors that dip you into negative thinking and undermine your conviction in your potential to build holistic riches. Naysayers might come in the shape of spouses, exes, ordinary friends, and family members. Toxic relationships are damaging to holistic wealth; toxic individuals want to lock you into a narrative in which you become fearful of your objectives and afraid of not being good enough, which produces a loop of negativity.

Your thinking patterns may be a fountain of plenty to live life on your terms. But negative talk and self-doubt are a drain on your inner energies. Our connections constitute the cornerstone of our life. Strong supporting connections boost our pleasure and contribute to holistic riches. However, certain relationships might generate tension and badly affect our mental well-being.

Below Are 5 Ways Toxic Relationships Can Hurt Your Ability To Achieve Holistic Wealth:

1. They Detract You From Achieving Your Goals

Naysayers are confidence-bashers and goal-destroyers who will fling you into a state of perplexity, where you begin to second-guess your ambitions and waste crucial time procrastination. This leads to feeling overwhelmed and immobilized – and will hinder you from taking calculated risks – a vital component of obtaining holistic riches. Measured risks are a key part of holistic prosperity. They are catalysts for movement, development, and change in our lives. They convey not just daring to act in the face of uncertainty, but also a degree of confidence in managing risk.

2. They Ruin Your Self-Confidence

When we engage with positive individuals – who adopt a holistic wealth attitude, it drives resilience, self-confidence, empathy for others; respect for variety; and an openness to trying new things and being imaginative and creative. On the other side, toxic relationships kill your self-confidence and make you second-guess all your judgments and choices.

3. They Keep you Stuck in the Past

Do you recall that friend or Ex that will not allow you to move on from the mistake you committed in the past? Or the buddy that makes pronouncements on your future since you are suddenly a single parent with kids? Either way, they keep you bound in a specific mold - based on some preconceived assumption that your present position (or your prior experiences) are somehow connected to your capacity to attain your objectives.

4. You Feel You Need to Give Up Your Identity

If you are around friends or in a relationship where you can't be yourself - that's a warning sign. Being your real self without worrying about "fitting in" - is a very essential element of self-care. Imagine having to put your actual sentiments by the wayside because someone doesn't care enough to listen to you. Or feeling like you have to put on a new character to fit into a specific circle or group? On some level, this robs you of walking in your mission and being uniquely you.

5. They Encourage Mindless Behaviour That Leads to Stunted Growth & Potential.

Whether is mindless shopping, thoughtless eating, or another harmful habit - toxic relationships foster poor behavior which may deprive you of the opportunity to reach holistic riches. If you are continuously feeling forced to spend money you don't have – and breaking your budget – to retain a specific connection or relationship – then that's a negative indicator. Similarly, if that individual sabotages your fitness, nutrition, or other lifestyle or professional objectives then is hard to realize your maximum potential.

Our spiritual, bodily, mental, and emotional states are deeply connected. Letting rid of limiting ideas that contribute to melancholy, procrastination, and mindlessness is crucial.

6. Don't engage in negative self-talk.

Life is fundamentally fraught with challenges that are beyond our control: the circumstances we are born into, unanticipated occurrences, situations we are unprepared for, etc. But there are certain things we can control over and among them are our ideas and how we care for ourselves. Life has enough hurdles, we do not need to make things more difficult for ourselves and inflict more agony than life already delivers. One thing you can do for yourself that does not cost one dime and offers big benefits is to give yourself a break. Negative thoughts and sentiments inflict enormous harm, visible and unseen, so it's crucial to keep them to a minimum. That's much easier said than done, but here are three techniques to help interrupt negative thoughts and self-talk.

When it comes to psychology and money, the only thing worse than surrounding yourself with losers is thinking you're a loser.

Do you say things like, “My work is too demanding,” “It’s not my fault,” or “I’m not clever enough?”

Say it enough, and you’ll believe it.

“When you allow negativity to govern your thoughts, you are wiring your brain for failure,” Corley stated. “You’ll have no shot in life at breaking out of your existing financial or living situations. These negative ideas will become beliefs that behave like computer programs.

We all have this inner critic. At times this tiny voice may be beneficial and keep us driven toward goals–like when it warns us that what we're going to eat isn't healthy or that what we're about to do may not be prudent. However, this voice may frequently be more damaging than beneficial, especially when it falls into the area of extreme negativity. This is known as negative self-talk, and it can knock us down.

Negative self-talk is something that most of us encounter from time to time, and it comes in various forms. It also produces enormous stress, not just to ourselves but to everyone around us if we're not cautious. Here's everything you need to know about negative self-talk and its consequences on your body, your mind, your life, and your loved ones.

Consequences of Negative Self-Talk

Negative self-talk may influence us in some fairly detrimental ways. One large-scale research indicated that rumination and self-blame about unfavorable occurrences were connected to an increased risk of mental health disorders.

Focusing on negative thoughts may lead to lower motivation as well as higher emotions of powerlessness. This sort of critical inner conversation has also been related to depression, so it's something to change.

Negative self-talk may lead to a lessened capacity to identify possibilities, as well as a decreased likelihood to capitalize on these chances. This implies that the heightened experience of stress arises from both the perception and the changes in behavior that occur from it. Other implications of negative self-talk might include:

Limited thinking: The more you tell yourself you can't accomplish something, the more you believe it.

Perfectionism: You come to sincerely think that "excellent" isn't as good as "perfect," and that perfection is possible. In contrast, simple high performers tend to fare better than their perfectionistic counterparts since they are typically less stressed and are content with a job well done. They don't tear it apart and attempt to home in on what might have been better.

Emotions of depression: Some studies have indicated that negative self-talk might contribute to a worsening of feelings of depression. If left uncontrolled, this might be highly destructive.

Relationship challenges: Whether the continual self-criticism makes you look needy and insecure or you transfer your negative self-talk into more general bad behaviors that affect others, a lack of communication and even a "playful" amount of criticism may take a toll.

One of the most apparent problems of negative self-talk is that it's not positive. This seems basic, yet research has proven that positive self-talk is a strong predictor of success.

For example, one research on athletes evaluated four distinct forms of self-talk (instructional, motivational, positive, and negative) and found that positive self-talk was the biggest predictor of performance.

People didn't need to remind themselves how to accomplish anything as much as they needed to persuade themselves that they are doing something amazing and that others notice it as well.

How to Minimize Negative Self-Talk

There are various techniques to lessen self-talk in your everyday life. Different tactics work better for different individuals, so try a few on and find which ones are most beneficial for you.

1. Catch Your Critic.

Learn to detect when you're being self-critical so you can begin to quit. For example, observe when you say things to yourself that you wouldn't say to a close friend or a kid.

2. Remember That Thoughts and Feelings Aren't Always Reality.

Thinking bad things about oneself may seem like keen observations, but your ideas and emotions about yourself can not be regarded as facts. Your ideas may be warped like everyone else's, vulnerable to prejudices and the effect of your emotions.

3. Give Your Inner Critic a Nickname

There was once a "Saturday Night Live" character known as Debbie Downer. She would find the bad in every scenario. If your inner critic has this questionable ability as well, you might tell yourself, "Debbie Downer is doing her thing again.

When you conceive of your inner critic as a force outside of yourself and even give it a silly moniker, it's not just more simple to recognize that you don't have to agree, but it becomes less scary and easier to see how ludicrous some of your critical ideas may be.

4. Contain Your Negativity

If you find yourself participating in negative self-talk, it helps to restrict the harm that a critical inner voice may create by just allowing it to criticize select items in your life, or be negative for only an hour in your day. This sets a limit on how much negativity may flow from the scenario.

5. Change Negativity to Neutrality
When engaged in negative self-talk, you may be able to catch yourself, but it may often be tough to push yourself to halt a train of thinking in its tracks. It's generally considerably simpler to modify the intensity of your words. "I can't bear this" becomes, "This is tough." "I dislike..." becomes, "I don't like..." and even, "I don't favor..." When your self-talk employs more soothing language, much of its negative effect is subdued as well.
6. Cross-Examine Your Inner Critic
One of the destructive characteristics of negative self-talk is that it typically goes unchecked. After all, if it's going on in your brain, people may not be aware of what you're saying and therefore can't tell you how incorrect you are.
It's a lot better to notice your negative self-talk and question how accurate it is. The great majority of negative self-talk is an exaggeration, and calling yourself on this may help to take away its destructive impact.

7. Think Like a Friend

When our inner critic is at its worst, it might sound like our deadliest adversary. Often we'll say things to ourselves in our minds that we'd never say to a buddy. Why not reverse this and—when you find yourself speaking harshly in your head—make it a point to envision yourself saying this to a beloved friend?

If you know you wouldn't say it this way, think about how you'd express your views with a good friend or what you'd want a good friend to say to you. This is an excellent approach to changing your self-talk in general.

8. Shift Your Perspective

Sometimes looking at things, in the long run, might enable you to see that you may be putting too large a focus on something. For example, you may ask yourself whether anything you're outraged over will truly matter in five years or even one.

Another technique to adjust perspective is to pretend that you are panning out and looking at your issues from a vast distance. Even thinking of the world as a globe and of yourself as a little, tiny individual on this globe might remind you that most of your troubles aren't as huge as they appear. This may frequently lessen the negativity, dread, and urgency in negative self-talk.

9. Say It Aloud

Sometimes when you find yourself having negative things in your head, merely stating them out might help. Telling a trusted buddy what you're thinking about may frequently lead to a nice chuckle and put a light on how ludicrous some of our negative self-talk can be. Other times, it may at least provide support.

Even tossing certain negative self-talk words around under your breath might remind you how absurd and impractical they seem. This will remind you to give yourself a break.

10. Stop That Thought

For others, merely stopping negative ideas in their tracks might be therapeutic. This is known as "thought-stopping" and might take the form of snapping a rubber band around your wrist, imagining a stop sign, or just moving to another idea when a negative one enters your head. This may be useful with recurrent or excessively critical thoughts such as, "I'm no good," or, "I'll never be able to accomplish this," for example.

11. Replace the Bad With Some Good

This is one of the finest approaches to countering negative self-talk: Replace that with something better. Take a negative notion and replace it with something uplifting that's equally truthful.

Repeat until you find yourself having to do it less and less frequently. This works well with most negative habits: substituting unhealthy food with nutritious food, for example. It's a terrific method to build a more optimistic way of thinking about yourself and life.

www.ingramcontent.com/pod-product-compliance
Lightning Source LLC
LaVergne TN
LVHW010607160826
845677LV00013B/3298

* 9 7 9 8 8 4 4 4 5 4 9 1 2 *